GW01458964

I SAW IT
OUT THERE

VOLUME 5

Compiled and rewritten
by Tom Lyons

I SAW IT OUT THERE, VOLUME 5

Copyright © 2025 Tom Lyons

All rights reserved. No part of this may be reproduced without the author's prior consent, except for brief quotes used in reviews.

All information and opinions expressed in *I Saw It Out There, Volume 5* are the personal perspectives and experiences of those generous enough to submit them. Tom Lyons does not purport that the information presented in this book is based on accurate, current, or valid scientific knowledge.

Acknowledgments

It's no easy task for people to discuss their encounters with cryptids. I want to thank the many good people who took the time and energy to put their experiences into writing.

Some of the following names were altered to protect people's privacy.

Would you like to see your report in an issue of *I Saw It Out There*?

If so, all you have to do is type up a summary of your experience and email it to Tom Lyons at:

Living.Among.Bigfoot@gmail.com

Special Offer
If you submit a report and it is accepted, you will receive an exclusive paperback copy signed by Tom shortly after the book is released. If you'd like to participate in that offer, please include your mailing address in the email.

Contents

Report #1

I've hunted alone and camped alone more times than most. But my encounter reminded me I'm not as tough as I once thought.

It started like any other solo trip. Just me, a tent, and a two-mile trail that leads up into the mountains. I'd been going up there for many years. You don't go up there for phone service or views. You go to be alone.

The weather was perfect. Chilly enough to keep the bugs down, clear skies, stars bright as spotlights. I set up my little canvas tent around dusk, just where the trail bends near an old dry creek bed. Made a small fire, ate jerky and trail mix, and listened to the owls stir.

By 11, I was zipped into my sleeping bag, drowsy from the cold and the quiet. I remember closing my eyes to the sound of crickets and marsupials arguing with one another.

But then I heard a whistling that sounded too human to come from any woodland critter. It was slow and sweet, almost like a lullaby. But there was definitely something off about it. The notes circled in a way no bird or animal I knew ever did. And it was moving.

Then it circled my tent. I could hear it move clockwise, like someone was walking around me, always just outside the fabric wall. It got a little louder near the back, then softer near the front. Like a carousel of sound.

I didn't breathe. My knife was in my boot, but that might as well have been across the state. I didn't dare move. I just listened.

Then, the whistling stopped. And there was dead silence. It lasted for maybe thirty seconds.

And then there was a crunch. It sounded like a single step right outside my tent.

My whole body locked up. My mouth went dry. I thought about

unzipping the tent and jumping out, but some instinct warned me not to. Not only because I was scared, but because I didn't want to see what was out there.

That was the worst part. I *knew* something was out there, but I didn't want eyes on it. Not then. Not ever.

The step never came again. No more whistling. After maybe five minutes, the night sounds returned like someone had flipped a switch.

I wasn't able to sleep. I just laid there with my heart hammering until the sky turned gray.

Initially, I packed up fast. I didn't even eat. Just rolled everything up and hiked back down the trail without stopping. I kept looking over my shoulder like some city slicker, spooking at chipmunks and shadows. Eventually I made it to the car and didn't relax until I was back on pavement with the trees behind me.

It took me a few weeks to tell anyone. Finally, over coffee at the diner, I mentioned it to a friend who'd grown up in the same area.

I told her about the whistling.

She immediately looked like she had seen a ghost.

"I've heard that before," she replied.

"When?" I asked.

"When I was a kid. My granddad told me stories about it. He called it *The Whistler*. Said it used to haunt the hills.

I forced a laugh. "You're shitting me, right?"

But her face said she wasn't.

I never went back up to that area. Whatever that thing was, I don't think it was trying to scare me. It was just *there*, doing whatever it does, whistling its little tune like it always has. Long before I showed up. Long after I left.

Some things out there don't want to be seen. Some things just want to be heard. And they'll make sure you remember the sound.

Report #2

I've loved fishing since I first started when I was six. My daddy used to say I could cast a line before I could read a single word. Even now, thirty-odd years later, it's still where I go when I need quiet.

There's a lake I frequently go to in my hometown. It's the kind of lake where you can catch a good bass and maybe a sunburn. I went out early, just after sunrise. The lake was still, quiet. One of those mornings where even the bugs hadn't woken up yet. I had my usual setup: lawn chair, thermos of coffee, and tackle box. I picked a spot near the far end of the lake, past the last boat ramp, where the shore gets muddy. That's where I've always had the best luck.

I remember the first hour was slow. No bites, just ripples. Then, about an hour later, my line snagged. Not a tug. Not a bite. A snag. Like I'd hooked a log. I started reeling, figuring I'd latched onto some garbage. I wouldn't have been surprised if it was just an old tire.

But this thing pulled back. Heavy, and weirdly limp. It took some effort, but I finally dragged it in. It was a jacket. A black, soaking-wet canvas jacket, heavy as hell. It looked like it'd been submerged a long time, but not long enough to rot. I thought that was strange.

I laid it out on the ground, water pooling around it. It smelled a bit like mold and copper. The zipper was stuck, but I worked it open. Inside was something I'll never forget.

Folded neatly, like someone had taken real care, was what looked like skin. Human skin, and the skin. It was pale, soft, and had a pinkish hue. It was fresh and stitched at the edges like a suit.

I staggered back. Nearly threw up my coffee. I poked it with my knife. It gave, like real flesh.

I should've taken a picture. But I didn't. I couldn't. Because as I stood there, catching my breath, I noticed something there was no blood. Not on the skin. Not in the jacket. No stains, no fluids. Just clean, folded human skin, stitched together with black thread.

I dropped the knife. Grabbed the edge of the jacket to move it, just to get it out of the light.

That's when the skin twitched. Not a lot. But it really did move.

I backed away and didn't stop until I was at my truck. I drove home, hands shaking, throat dry. I didn't know what I'd seen. My mind kept trying to explain how that thing had gotten there.

The next morning, I went back to the lake. I had to.

But the jacket was gone.

But since then, I can't stop thinking about it. About the black stitching along the back, like it was made for someone to wear.

And about the way it twitched.

It's a local legend that the lake is bottomless in one spot near the far edge. And every time I drive past the lake, I see an unfamiliar tall figure standing out near the bank.

I haven't been back to fish since, and I don't think I ever will.

Report #3

I was eleven when I first saw it. We lived just past the church and before the road turns gravel and disappears into farmland. Our house sat across from Denton's cornfield, a hundred acres of tall, whispering stalks that ran all the way to the tree line. In summer, the corn grew thick and higher than a grown man, my father used to say.

The sightings started in July of 89. I was up late, trying to fall asleep while my brother snored in the bunk above.

That's when I saw what looked like glowing eyes.

I had glanced out the window without thinking, just something my brain did when it got bored. The cornfield was pitch black. But in the middle of that blackness were two glowing dots, just above the height of the corn, not moving.

At first, I thought it might be a machine. Denton had a harvester with bright lights.

But then it moved just enough for me to see the outline behind the eyes.

The silhouette was shaped like a person, but not quite. Too narrow at the waist. Shoulders hunched forward. The arms hung long and low. And the head tilted just a bit too far.

The next morning, I checked the field with my brother but didn't find anything. Just rows of corn, swaying in the wind like always.

But the next night, it was there again in the same spot.

Every night, at some point, it appeared, never making a sound. Just standing above the corn.

I sketched it in my notebook. Just the shape of it. I didn't know what else to do. I couldn't describe it well, not even to myself. It was always just a little too far and a little too dark.

One night, I worked up the nerve to shine my flashlight toward it. Just for a second. The beam hit the corn but didn't reach the eyes. Still, the thing responded. It turned. Not away from me but toward me. Like it had noticed me for the first time.

I dropped the flashlight and crawled into bed, heart pounding, blankets pulled to my chin like they could save me.

It took just a few slow steps sideways, back and forth behind the corn. I could see the stalks swaying where it walked, like something big brushing past.

I told my mom I thought someone was in the field at night. She didn't know what to make of it but didn't want to believe me.

A week later, the eyes looked closer. Not by much. Just a foot or two forward. Still above the corn. Still motionless. But closer.

Each night after that, they came closer.

Until one night they were at the edge of the field. No more distance. No more rows between us. The shape tilted its head. And then, for the first time, it stepped *out of the corn.*

What I saw next, I still don't have words for. Just the sense that something unusual had entered the world and chosen me to see it.

I screamed.

My mom ran in. By the time she flipped on the light, it was gone.

The next morning, the corn was gone. Not cut. Not harvested. It had completely vanished.

How?

Report #4

My dad used to say the forest has its own memory. If you respect it, it'll give back. If you push it too far, it'll push back harder.

That morning in late November, I wasn't thinking about any of that. It had snowed the night before, just enough to muffle sound and leave clear tracks. That's perfect for hunting. I parked off the service road and hiked in before dawn. I had my .308 slung over my shoulder, thermos in my pack, and a tag burning a hole in my pocket.

Much sooner than I had anticipated, I spotted hoofprints bigger than most, leading down toward a frozen creek bed. I followed them as quietly as possible.

I reached the edge of a clearing and almost couldn't believe it. There, standing in the snow, was the elk.

At first, it looked ordinary. But then I saw its front legs bent backward at the knee. It wasn't just a limp. The whole joint structure was reversed, like the anatomy had been flipped inside out. Same with the back legs. It walked like a marionette, limbs bending in ways no living thing should.

My first thought wasn't fear. It was confusion. Then instinct took over. I raised my rifle. Scoped in.

Even with the deranged legs, it looked like an elk otherwise. The coat was darker than I had seen before, but I didn't think too hard about that. I lined up a shot behind the shoulder, exhaled, and squeezed.

The shot echoed through the woods.

The elk flinched. Not from pain but from surprise, like it noticed something brush past it. It didn't drop. Didn't even stagger.

The bullet *went through*. I saw it. Snow kicked up behind it. Blood didn't.

It turned and looked straight at me. It was like it knew what I'd done and wanted me to understand something back.

Then it walked off. Smooth and slow, each backwards-bending limb rising high in the snow and touching down without a sound.

I stood there, stunned, breath fogging in front of me.

Eventually I lowered my rifle and backed away. I didn't track it because I didn't care to try for a second shot. Something in me knew that would be a mistake.

I hiked out, slower than before, every snapped twig behind me making my skin crawl. When I reached the truck,

I sat behind the wheel for ten minutes before I could start the engine.

That night I cleaned my gun twice, even though it was already spotless.

The next morning, I went back to check the area. I found the spot I'd fired from.

There were no tracks leading away. Just one trail of hoofprints leading *in*, then nothing at all. Like it had disappeared.

I found my shell casing but no blood. No hair. No sign of injury. I walked the perimeter, even checked the brush line. Still nothing.

I've seen the woods differently ever since. Before, I knew where the danger was. I used to fear slippery ice, angry bears, stupid people, etc. But this creature changed my perspective. It looked like something I should understand, but I didn't. That's the part that still gets me.

How easily it wore the shape of something familiar. How close it let me get. How it let me shoot. And how it walked away unharmed and untouched.

To claim your free eBooks, visit
www.LivingAmongBigfoot.com

and click the FREE BOOKS tab!

Report #5

We weren't supposed to be out there. The trail we *were* on was closed off at the overlook due to a mudslide earlier that spring. But Jake had heard something about an old fire tower out there, which he wanted to climb. And like idiots, we followed him.

We parked and took the road up past an old cattle fence. Within half an hour, the trail disappeared into wild brush. That's when we saw the red cloth.

It was tied to a pine branch, fluttering just above eye level. Bright red. Torn at the ends like someone had ripped it by hand.

"It's a trail marker," Jake said, pointing. "People do that all the time off-path."

We followed it.

Another red cloth appeared a hundred yards ahead. Then another. Always tied about the same height, always just visible from the last one. It was weird, yeah, but not unheard of. We figured it was someone's way of marking a hunting trail or a shortcut through the woods.

But it wasn't long before the mood shifted.

That's when Lacey said, "Does something smell off to you guys?"

She was right. There was a stink in the air. It smelled like something had been rotting for years, for lack of a better description. Jake suggested that maybe a deer or raccoon died nearby, but I thought it was so much worse than that.

Soon, we found the next "marker."

This one wasn't tied to a branch. It was nailed to the trunk of a cedar. Still red, still ragged, but thicker than cloth.

I don't know what made me touch it, but the second my fingers pressed into it, I knew. It wasn't fabric. It was flesh. It was wet, rubbery, and warm.

Lacey gagged and backed away. Jake squinted at it like he was trying to convince himself he was wrong.

I already knew the shape. The width. The tapering point. The muscle fibers torn at one end like it had been yanked out.

It was a tongue, likely human.

We should've turned around. But the trail kept going, and the red "flags" appearing.

It was like we were in some kind of trance.

More tongues lined the path, nailed to bark, draped like streamers. All of them human.

Jake stopped walking first. "Listen," he whispered.

And we did.

"Someone's hurt," Lacey soon said, having heard something that I hadn't.

"No," I whispered, thinking she was about to follow the sound.

We backed away, stepping carefully, retracing the trail of tongues.

That's when we realized we weren't going back the same way.

It was as if the forest had changed. The ground didn't match what we came through. And the tongues were still there, but in different places. And I could tell they were new ones.

Jake looked like he had seen a ghost. "We're going in circles."

"I think we're being led by something supernatural," I replied.

Suddenly, we sprinted through the brush and branches, trying not to scream.

Eventually, we burst into a clearing. In the middle stood an old, rusted fire tower like Jake had heard about. On the lowest step, crouched like an animal, was a figure. It had long limbs, no clothes, and skin so white that it was like it had never seen the sun.

It turned toward us, and Lacey immediately screamed. Jake pulled her back.

We continued running like our lives depended on it and somehow made it out of the woods alive. We still don't know what that entity was, or whether it had anything to do with the human tongues.

Report #6

I deliver medical supplies across three counties, looping between hospitals, rural clinics, and urgent care offices. I'd been running that route for seven years, long enough to know which backroads saved time and which ones flooded when it rained. That night, I was coming back from a late drop. The sun had set hours earlier.

My truck's AC was broken again, so I had the windows down. I was about twenty miles from home when I noticed it.

That was when I got an unexplainable strange feeling that caused me to glance in the rearview mirror.

There was a figure sitting in the middle of the backseat. It was still as stone.

I nearly drove off the road. I swerved, yanked the wheel back, slammed the brakes. Came to a screeching stop halfway into the shoulder, heartbeat thudding in my ears.

I looked again. They were still there.

It was a woman, though I wasn't sure at first. She had shoulder-length hair, and she was crying. She covered her face like most people do while teary-eyed.

But it wasn't long before I realized her mouth appeared to be sewn shut.

Not metaphorically. Not with tape or cloth. It was stitched. Black thread drawn through the lips in crude, angry Xs, as if someone had done it with no care for pain.

I opened the door and jumped out, ran around the truck, ripped open the back door.

She was gone. The seat was empty.

I checked the floor. The other door. The bed of the truck. Nothing.

I stood there in the dark, trying to slow my pulse. Trying to understand what I had just experienced.

I told myself I must've dozed off at the wheel. Hallucinated it. That's all. I got back in the cab and drove.

Report #7

I regularly hike because it's the only place I feel truly away from smartphones, traffic, small talk, etc. It's usually nothing but trees and the sky.

That's how I ended up a few miles outside of Sycamore, Kentucky. I'd found an old forestry map in a used bookstore the week before, and there was this unmarked trail curving deep into the hills where I suspect no one had built anything since the Depression. I was curious to see what was out there.

The trail was overgrown but walkable, like no one had been through in years but the land hadn't quite absorbed it yet. The hike began as serene as any, but then something changed.

One second, I was listening to a woodpecker hammering out some Morse code two trees over. The next second, it was almost as if I had lost my hearing. It was like the whole forest had been vacuum-sealed.

And then I realized I couldn't even hear my own breathing. That startled me, so I exhaled on purpose several times.

I finally heard it but it was muffled, like the sound was getting caught in something before reaching my ears. Like the forest wasn't letting most of the noise pass through.

Then I noticed something up ahead, maybe thirty yards away. I saw it walk between two pines, but I wasn't quite sure it was a person. The only thing I could tell for sure was that it was on two legs.

However, it wasn't long after spotting the being that I noticed the antlers. I don't know how I missed them at first. They were large, twisted things that curved like driftwood and seemed too heavy for its head. They scraped the lower branches as it moved. But the worst part wasn't the antlers.

It was slightly hunched but it had to be close to seven feet tall. And its skin was the color of old bark, patchy in places.

Then the thing raised its arm, and it pointed at the ground in front of me.

I looked down to find something round half-buried in the dead leaves.

It was a human skull. And I could tell it wasn't old, either. Bits of scalp still clung to it. The brown hair was matted.

I stepped back, which caused the antlered creature to flinch.

It didn't charge. It was more like it was being pulled forward by something just behind it.

That was when I turned and ran. I should've done that much sooner but logic doesn't always work when you see something that isn't supposed to exist.

As soon as I fled, it seemed like the trail twisted under me like it didn't want me to leave.

At one point, I stumbled down a slope and hit the ground hard. My knee lit up in pain, but I didn't stop. I pushed through the underbrush, thorns ripping my sleeves. I looked over my shoulder and saw that it was closer.

It didn't rush. It just followed like it had all the time in the world.

When I finally broke through the tree line, the noise returned immediately. It hit me like a slap.

Fortunately, that *thing* didn't cross into the open. I still feel overwhelming gratitude whenever I reflect on how I made it out of there alive.

A week later, I saw a flyer at the gas station. "MISSING HIKER." The photo was of a younger guy with brown hair.

Report #8

We moved to Washington Island, Wisconsin, in the fall of '94. Just me, my wife Beth, and our daughter Katie, who had just turned five. If you're unfamiliar with the island, you can only reach it via ferry. Our house was old, creaky, and built in that stubborn way mid-century homes are. It had thick wood beams, narrow crawl spaces, and nothing was square or leveled. But it had a big yard and a wide porch that wrapped around the front, and it truly felt like home at the start.

The first couple of months were uneventful. We unpacked, repainted the walls, got used to the quiet. Katie spent most of her time outside, playing with her dolls beneath the porch or drawing pictures in the dust. She liked it there. She regularly reminded us that it was her "secret fort."

We didn't think much of it until she started talking about a man who Beth nor I had encountered.

One evening in late October, Katie came inside, dirty-kneed and wide-eyed.

"Daddy," she said, tugging at my shirt. "The man under the porch was talking to me again."

I half-laughed, thinking she was playing make-believe. "Is that right? What was he talking to you about?"

"He said I shouldn't tell you," Katie replied.

Beth and I exchanged a look. We chalked it up to imagination. Kids say weird things, especially when they're that young and adjusting to a new place. I asked her to draw him, and she did: a stick figure with long arms and no clothes. "He has stringy hair," she said. "And dirty knees like mine."

We told her not to talk to strangers, even pretend ones, and left it at that.

A few days later, she brought it up again. Same story.

Only this time, she said he tried to give her a shiny rock. She showed it to me. It was shaped like a tear.

"Where'd you find this?" I asked.

"He slid it to me," Katie said. "His hands are big."

I got a flashlight and checked under the porch. I didn't expect to find anything, but something in her voice had unsettled me. I crouched down, clicked on the beam, and scanned the space.

I didn't see anything other than old boards, dry leaves, and cobwebs. I brushed it off. Probably found the rock out in the yard. Maybe made up the rest.

A few days later, I was in the garage when Beth screamed. I dropped the wrench and ran outside. She was standing at the edge of the porch, holding Katie tight.

"He was under there," Beth gasped. "He moved."

"What?"

"I saw *someone* crawling out from under the house. I thought it was a dog at first."

We grabbed a hammer and a kitchen knife, and I crouched again at the porch's edge. This time I didn't shine the flashlight.

I just listened.

It wasn't long before I heard something shuffle.

And before I could react, it burst out.

Crawling at first, crab-like, elbows grinding into the dirt. Then it stood, completely naked, covered in a coat of grime and hair. Its eyes were sunken deep, and its mouth opened wide in a gurgling holler. It was like something between a scream and a moan. Then it bolted.

Ran like an animal toward the trees.

Beth screamed again. I didn't chase it. I was too shocked to move.

We called the cops. A couple of them came out, stomped around under the porch, checked the woods. But they didn't find anything other than some scratch marks in the dirt and a clump of what might've been hair.

They asked Katie questions. She told them what she told us. "He lives under the porch. He doesn't like loud noises. He says he's old."

They chuckled over my daughter's comments. "Could be a transient," one of them said. "They pass through now and then. He was probably high and paranoid."

But Beth and I both knew what we saw.

That thing wasn't high.

And it didn't see entirely human.

After that, we sealed the porch. Nailed in boards. Poured gravel under there. Katie stopped playing outside. She didn't talk about him again.

We stayed in the house for about three more years. Nothing else happened.

The new owners never asked about the porch, so I never offered to explain. I was worried it would've freaked them out for no reason.

Report #9

We started our hike just after 9 a.m., and it was halfway up the incline that we found *it*.

My friend Ben was the first to see it. "Is that a deer?"

It was. Or had been. The body was half-submerged in leaves just off the trail, like it had collapsed mid-step. But something about it seemed off. The skin was intact, but the whole thing looked deflated, like a costume someone had worn and discarded. As far as we could tell, there were no ribs, no spine, no tension in the limbs. It was just slumped.

"That's gross," my other buddy, Tyler, muttered while crouching beside it. "Where could the bones have gone?"

He was right. There was no structure. You could've picked it up like a sleeping bag.

I knelt next to it. The fur was clean. No blood. No smell of rot. It was like it had been emptied out and left there.

But then I saw its eyes move a bit. The left one twitched toward me. It was clear that it was looking at me.

I nearly tripped over my own boots, as I rose.

"Let's get away from this thing," I said.

"Dude," Ben said. "I think it's still alive. How—"

"I don't care," I snapped. "Let's go."

That hollow body made my skin crawl. It was like it had been made for someone something else to wear. Like something had stepped inside, walked around for a while, then decided it didn't need it anymore.

Finally, wc agreed to leave it behind.

The forest felt different after that.

Tyler tried to joke about how maybe it was a taxidermy project gone wrong.

When I glanced over my shoulder, the deer's head had changed positions. It was angled slightly up now, toward the trail. And I knew for sure that it was looking at us.

Not long after that, we became unsure of where we were along the trail.

Ben checked the map twice, then his phone, but there was no cell signal.

Suddenly, Tyler threw up behind a stump but felt relief immediately after.

Eventually we ended up at the clearing where we had parked our vehicle, and we got the hell out of there.

I haven't hiked since. Honestly, I don't know whether I ever will again.

Report #10

I've lived in rural towns my whole life. First, I was in Tennessee, then Oklahoma, and now I'm in southern Illinois. We moved out here two years ago when we bought twenty acres of tall grass, and a long stretch of tree line that looked almost black in the distance no matter how bright the sun shone. The creaky hardwood floors made the dog bark every night for the first week.

The night it happened, I'd just finished repairing the back fence, and my back was killing me. Maggie and I were asleep, and our two kids, Josh and Emily, were tucked in down the hall. Everything was quiet.

Then something knocked on the front door.

I sat up in bed, heart already racing. Maggie stirred beside me. "What was that?"

Then Josh's voice called from the hallway. "Dad, I think someone's at the door."

I grabbed the baseball bat from under the bed and moved to the living room. Through the small window in the front door, I saw something that completely caught me off guard.

The top of its head nearly touched the doorframe. It had a narrow waist and even narrower chest.

The upper body was human-shaped, yes, but covered with black or dark brown fur. And sprouting from its head were two massive, curling horns resembling what you'd see on a goat.

Its face was long, animal-like, somewhere between goat and man, with wide black eyes that reflected light like a deer's. Its mouth opened, and I braced myself for some guttural screech.

But it didn't scream.

It *spoke.*

A low, rumbling voice poured from it in a language I couldn't understand. Not gibberish, though. This was something real and structured. It didn't raise its voice. Just stated something.

Then it went silent.

We all just stood there. I was on one side of the door while Maggie clutched the kids behind me, and that thing was on our porch.

And then it turned, walked down the steps, down the gravel path, back toward the tree line.

I didn't move until the thing was out of sight.

"Call the police," Maggie whispered.

They came about twenty minutes later. There were two deputies. Nice guys, both from the area. They checked for tracks. Found what they believed to be hoof prints.

"Could be a prank," one of the deputies said, not sounding convinced.

At two in the morning? Ten miles from anything?

They filed a report, offered to send a car by the next night. We thanked them. They left.

The next morning, I followed the prints. They went past the tree line, deeper into the woods. I didn't go far. Something in my gut said not to push my luck.

We told ourselves it was a one-time thing. But the kids started waking up at night. Saying they heard bells. Like small, tinny wind chimes, way off in the woods.

Then Emily started calling it "the Speaker."

When I asked why, she said, "Because it came to tell us something."

But she didn't know what it was. None of us did. That was a while back, and we haven't seen it since.

It already said what it came to say. Whatever that was.

If you ever find yourself out near rural southern Illinois, and you hear a knock in the middle of the night, don't open the door.

Visit My Digital Book Store

If you're looking for NEW reads, check out my digital store, www.TomLyonsBooks.com. Buying my books directly from me means you save money—because my store will always sell for less than big retailers. My store also offers sales, deals, bundles, and pre-order discounts you won't find anywhere else.

Visit my store now to get a FREE audiobook!

Report #11

I rented a cabin that sat at the edge of the woods, a single-story place with no neighbors, no Wi-Fi, and only one key, which was taped under the doormat when I arrived.

The solitude was worth it. You don't realize how loud the world is until it no longer is for you.

It was only my second night there that the VHS tape appeared. It was sitting dead center on the porch railing when I stepped out for coffee around 6 a.m., just as the mist was rising from the trees. It was a black cassette without a label or a case.

Initially, I figured it had been left by the last renter, and I just hadn't noticed it. Maybe someone dropped it. Maybe it had been inside and got kicked out by the cleaning service. But when I asked the property manager—some guy named Russ who only answered texts when he felt like it—he said no one had stayed there in two weeks.

I almost threw the tape away. But the curiosity got me.

There was an old combo TV/VCR in the living room, a dusty little cube with rabbit ears and a warped screen. I plugged it in, slid in the tape, and hit play.

The screen flickered with static. Then it cut to black-and-white footage of a man sleeping. That man was me. The footage was of me lying in bed the night before.

The angle was fixed, high in the corner like a security camera. Just hours of footage of me sleeping, unaware.

The cabin had no cameras. I'd looked. No smoke detector with a blinking red light. No blinking lens in the corner. I checked again anyway.

I tore through the bedroom, the closet, even under the bed, but found nothing. No wires. No devices. The place was clean.

And yet the footage existed.

That night, I barricaded the door. Shoved a chair under the knob, locked every window, and left the porch light on. I didn't sleep much. Every time I closed my eyes, I imagined a lens focusing in the dark.

By morning, I was jumpy and wired. But there was no sign anyone had come near.

But when I stepped outside, there was another tape. It was in the same spot, dead center on the porch railing.

This one had a sticky note on it: **2**.

I didn't watch it right away. Part of me wanted to burn it, toss it in the fire and forget any of this happened. But some dark, gnawing curiosity made me push it into the VCR.

Me, again.

But this time, I wasn't sleeping. I was lying in bed, motionless with my eyes open. I was staring at something just out of frame. I looked terrified.

The tape played in real time. Minutes passed. I never moved. Then, at the thirty-four-minute mark, a hand entered the frame.

It was pale and thin, reaching toward me from off-camera.

I didn't react. Didn't flinch. I just kept staring likc I was too scared to scream.

The hand hovered above my face for a full minute before the footage ended.

I rewound it and watched it again. The tape had constant room noise, but I never heard the door open.

That was the moment I decided to leave.

I packed everything and got the hell out of there as quickly as possible.

Report #12

If you live long enough on a farm, you think you've seen it all. Cows giving birth breech, foxes raiding the henhouse, raccoons getting bold enough to paw at your kitchen screen door. You figure nothing out here can surprise you.

Well, it turned out I was wrong about that.

It was early August when we'd had a stretch of thunderstorms roll through, and the roof on my old barn had started leaking for what felt like the twentieth time. I told myself I'd climb up and patch it before it got worse.

That night, I was in the house having supper when I heard something slam in the barn. Not a little creak or thud. I really mean something *slammed*.

I grabbed a flashlight and headed out. I'd owned this place for close to thirty years. Nothing about it scared me.

Until I opened the door, and I immediately noticed the smell. It wasn't manure or wet hay. Those smells are part of a farmer's life. This was sharp and sour.

"Damn coons," I muttered. "Better not have torn into the feed again."

I swept the flashlight across the floor. Dust swirled in the beam. The stalls were empty. No raccoons. No movement at all.

Then I heard a soft rustle above me, so I tilted the light upward. The rafters were full of glowing eyes. There had to be dozens of them.

Glowing a yellowish green in the beam, they blinked almost in unison, but not like owls or raccoons or any night animal I knew.

I froze. My mind tried to make sense of it. I wondered if it could be bats. But I also knew bats don't have glowing eyes.

"Get outta here!" I shouted.

But they didn't budge. They just kept staring.

Then, one of the figures detached itself from the rafters and scuttled down the post like a spider, limbs bending too many ways.

When it hit the ground, I finally saw it in the light. It definitely wasn't a raccoon. It wasn't anything I recognized.

Its skin was hairless and stretched thin over a spindly frame. Its arms ended in narrow hands with needle-like fingers. Its head was round, and its mouth was wide and lipless, packed with tiny, jagged teeth like a catfish.

It hissed as it lunged.

It sank its teeth into my forearm before I got a chance to swing my flashlight at it.

The pain was white-hot, tearing through me like fire. I shouted and slammed my arm against the nearest post, hard enough to make my teeth rattle.

The thing let go with a squeal.

Then, like someone had fired a pistol, the rafters exploded with movement.

All of the spindly creatures rushed for the open door. They moved on all fours, their limbs bending at awful angles, claws clicking against the boards. The sound still haunts me. Within seconds, the barn was empty.

I staggered back, clutching my arm. Blood ran down to my wrist. By the time I stumbled outside, the creatures were gone. I wrapped my arm with my bandana and made for the house.

In the morning, I checked the barn. There was no sign of the creatures or anything at all. Except for the bite, which consisted of two neat rows of punctures on my arm.

I called my doctor to tell him that a strange animal bit me. He ended up giving me a shot but didn't ask many questions.

The bite still hasn't healed completely. The skin around it looks weirdly gray, but at least I feel fine.

If anyone has any clue regarding what those creatures could've been, please let Tom Lyons know as soon as possible.

Report #13

Camping has always been one of my favorite things to do. So when my friend Luke asked me to join him and his girlfriend Hannah for a weekend out near Luray, Virginia, I said yes without thinking twice.

We drove up on a Friday afternoon, weaving through the Blue Ridge until the cell signal dropped to nothing and the only sound left was the crunch of tires on gravel. The campsite was small and quiet, just off a narrow trail in Shenandoah. It was perfect.

The first night was uneventful. We set up the tent, got a fire going, ate our foil dinners, and passed a flask around until the stars overhead blurred. I slept better than I had in weeks.

But it was the second night that I'll never forget. I woke sometime after midnight to a sound.

Not loud. Just a soft *shhhk*, like fabric brushing against itself.

For a moment I thought it was the wind shifting the tent walls, but the air outside was still. I held my breath and listened.

There it was again.

Shhhk. Shhhk.

This time it came with a faint crunch.

I nudged Luke, who was snoring beside me. "Hey, you hear that?"

He mumbled something and rolled over.

I sat up and glanced at Hannah. She was curled up on the other side, breathing slow and steady.

Then there was another noise that sounded even closer.

This wasn't a raccoon or deer. Whatever it was, it moved on two legs.

Then something brushed against the tent wall.

There was a shadow outside. It was long and thin, and stretched across the fabric. And then it leaned down to press its face against the tent.

At first, I only saw its outline while it just stayed there, pressed against the nylon like it wanted me to see it.

I didn't move a muscle.

The thing's head twitched like a bird.

Luke stirred. "What is it?" he muttered, still half-asleep.

I didn't answer.

The thing's hand brushed the tent. I saw long, thin fingers tracing along the seam. The tips pressed inward slightly, and the nylon dented.

I wanted to scream.

But Luke sat up. "What the hell are you doing?" he said, his voice groggy but sharp enough to carry.

The thing outside our tent went still.

Then, as suddenly as it appeared, it pulled back.

I heard footsteps retreating into the woods.

Luke grabbed the flashlight and unzipped the tent. I hissed, "Dude, don't!" but he'd already shoved his head out, beam slicing through the trees.

However, he didn't see anything. "Probably some loser trying to mess with us," he muttered.

But I knew that wasn't the case. This was definitely something else.

By sunrise, we'd packed up and took off.

I haven't been camping since.

Report #14

My house in Hastings was old—1910s construction, cracked plaster walls, and a crawlspace underneath that the realtor said had "good bones." For the first several months after I moved in, it felt like I'd made the right choice.

But then the scratching started. I'd been reading in bed when first I heard it. It was faint at first, but then it came again, louder, a sound from somewhere below the floorboards. It seemed like it was coming from the crawlspace.

I told myself it had to be mice or rats. After all, old houses were magnets for that sort of thing.

The sound stopped, I waited for a couple of minutes before finally setting the book down and turning out the light.

The next night, I heard it again. It kind of sounded like fingers dragging across wood.

Somehow, I mustered the courage to get out of bed and check things out.

The crawlspace entrance was in the laundry room, a square panel you had to pull up to access the dirt and beams below the house.

My heart raced as I pulled the panel free and crouched down. Cold air rose up from the dark. My flashlight beam caught on the bare earth and wooden supports, a web of cobwebs catching the light like threads of glass.

"Alright," I muttered. "Let's see what you are."

I lowered myself halfway through the opening, light scanning the space.

Something glinted, and I soon realized it was paper. A folded scrap, wedged between two beams, like it had been left there on purpose.

I shuffled forward and grabbed it.

On the outside, in blocky, almost childlike handwriting, were three words: Don't look again.

My stomach turned cold. I backed out fast, nearly smacking my head on the panel as I pulled myself into the laundry room.

I didn't even go back upstairs. I sat at the kitchen table until the sun came up, the note still clutched in my hand, trying to assess whether I was losing my mind.

I tried to be rational about it.

The handwriting looked too old to have been scribed recently.

And why "don't look again?"

Not "don't look." Not "stay out."

"Again." Like it knew I'd be there.

That night, I boarded up the crawlspace panel. Nailed it shut.

Then I went to bed, determined not to listen.

But I heard it anyway. And this time it wasn't coming from below. It was coming from the walls.

Something moving up, like it was dragging itself between the studs.

I stared at the ceiling, fists clenched, too afraid to breathe.

Then I heard it behind my headboard.

Then, all went silent.

The next morning, I called a pest control company.

"Probably squirrels," the guy said over the phone. "Or rats. They love old houses. We'll come by tomorrow."

"Make it today," I said.

He couldn't.

I ended up spending the day in town and didn't go back until sunset.

As I pulled into the driveway, I saw something odd. The boards over the crawlspace panel were gone.

Nails scattered across the floor like someone had pried them out, one by one.

I didn't go inside.

I drove straight to the motel on Route 6 and paid for three nights.

The pest guy said the house is empty. "Didn't see signs of critters," he told me over the phone. "But something's been moving dirt around under there. You been doing work?"

"No," I replied.

He paused. "It's probably nothing."

Mysteriously, the phenomenon stopped after the pest guy came by.

Report #15

I saw something crazy while I was driving west out of Marfa, Texas. I'd been helping my uncle fix up an old house outside of town. The road was straight, flat, and quiet. No cars, no lights, no towns for miles. I had the radio on low volume.

Suddenly, there was a figure up ahead on the shoulder.

Initially, I thought it was a hitchhiker. He was standing in the ditch just off the road, half-hidden by tall grass. As I got closer, he stepped out into the glow of my high beams.

He was a thin guy. Relatively tall, maybe six feet. He was barefoot, wearing a tattered sweater and jeans.

But it was his face that stuck with me. His eyes were absurdly wide.

I eased my foot off the gas. My first thought was to stop, to ask if he needed help. It can get cold out there at night.

But something about him made my gut clench. He didn't wave. Didn't stick out a thumb.

He just looked at me with a strange expression that's hard to explain.

I tapped the gas again. The car lurched forward. Fifty. Fifty-five.

In my rearview mirror, he was still standing there, small and distant in the red glow of my taillights.

That was when he dropped onto all fours and lunged into the road behind me.

"What the hell?"

He was running. On hands and feet. And he was keeping up with my vehicle.

I was doing fifty.

I watched in the mirror as his limbs pumped, his body nearly touching the asphalt.

I slammed my foot down. Sixty. Sixty-five. The car shuddered on the cracked pavement.

He didn't fall back. And he was *gaining*.

I punched the gas harder. Seventy. Seventy-five. The engine whined.

Then, without warning, he veered off the road. One leap, and he vanished into the scrub brush.

I didn't slow down. Not for a long time.

By the time I hit the next gas station, I was shaking so bad I could barely get the car in park.

I hope I never experience anything like that again.

Conclusion

Thanks for reading! If you want more, read *I Saw It Out There, Volume 6.*

Editor's Note

Before you go, I'd like to thank you for purchasing this book.
I know you had various books to choose from, but you took a chance on my content. Therefore, thanks for reading this one and sticking with it to the last page.

I'd like to ask you for a *tiny* favor: It would mean the world to me if you could leave a review wherever you purchased this book.

Your feedback will aid me in creating products you and many others will enjoy.

Mailing List Sign-Up Form

Don't forget to sign up for the newsletter email list. I promise I will not use it to spam you but to ensure you always receive the first word on any new releases, discounts, or giveaways! You only need to visit the following URL and enter your email address.

URL-
http://eepurl.com/dhnspT

I SAW IT OUT THERE: VOLUME 5

Social Media

Feel free to follow/reach out to me with questions or concerns on either Instagram or Twitter! I will do my best to follow back and respond to all comments.

Instagram:
@living_among_bigfoot

Twitter:
@AmongBigfoot

I SAW IT OUT THERE: VOLUME 5

About the Editor

A simple man at heart, Tom Lyons lived an ordinary existence for his first 52 years. Native to the great state of Wisconsin, he went through the motions of everyday life, residing near his family and developing a successful online business. The world he once knew would completely change shortly after moving out west, where he was confronted by the allegedly mythical species known as Bigfoot.

You can email him directly at:

Living.Among.Bigfoot@gmail.com

Printed in Dunstable, United Kingdom

68509672R00068